Beating The
Ruy Lopez

GM Andrew Soltis

Chess Digest, Inc.

Copyright © 1994 Andrew Soltis

ISBN: 0-87568-249-9

AUTHOR: Andrew Soltis
EDITOR: Ken Smith
COMPUTER TYPESET: Lou Hays
COVER: Elaine Smith
FINAL PROOF: Sid Pickard
DIAGRAMS: Sid Pickard
FINAL PREPARATION: Lou Hays

PUBLISHER: Chess Digest, Inc. ®, 1601 Tantor, Dallas, Texas 75229

Send the publisher $2.00 for the *New Chess Guide* that catalogs every chess book for general sale in the United States. You are given publishers, page counts, notation, and critical reviews. Also included is a free Chess Improvement Course for beginners up through Master level players.

TABLE OF CONTENTS

INTRODUCTION

Anyone who has ever suffered through the ordeal of defending a main line of the Ruy Lopez defense must wonder if there's an easier way. After 1.e4 e5 2.Nf3 Nc6 3.Bb5 a6 4.Ba4 Nf6 5.0-0 Be7 6.Re1 b5 7.Bb3 d6 Black seems doomed to what may be several hours of cautious maneuvering.

One of those maneuvers, after Black castles, is the agonizing redeployment of his e7-Bishop with ...Re8, then ...Bf8 followed, most likely, by ...g7-g6 and ...Bg7. In this way Black increases the pressure on the only target he has, the d4-pawn.

But, you're bound to wonder, why does Black fianchetto the damn Bishop at move 17 or 20 when he can do it at move three? Good question.

This book explores the increasingly popular Fianchetto Defense to the Ruy Lopez. To play this defense you must be prepared to accept some odd-looking pawn structures and even make some rare pawn sacrifices. But the rewards can be substantial. Black often begins the middlegame with superior activity for his minor pieces and Rooks - a rarity for the Ruy Lopez.

The idea of fianchettoing Black's f8-Bishop had been tried against the Ruy Lopez at several points in the early history of the Spanish Game. A typical move order was **1.e4 e5 2.Nf3 Nc6 3.Bb5 Nge7 4.c3 g6 5.d4 Bg7 6.0-0 d6 7.d5 a6 8.Bd3 Nb8 9.c4 h6 10.Nc3 g5 11.Ne1 Ng6 12.Ne2 Nf4** as in Paulsen-Neumann, Baden-Baden 1870. One bit of irony here is that Paulsen was the originator of an offshoot of the Vienna Game (1.e4 e5 2.Nc3 Nf6 3.g3) - which is the reversed version of the Fianchetto Defense Lopez.

It was Wilhelm Steinitz who put the muscles into this variation. Steinitz sprang his conception on an unsuspecting chess world at the great London tournament of 1883. Having already tried most every other third move for Black, he gave his endorsement to 3...g6 beginning with:

George Henry Mackenzie-Wilhelm Steinitz
London 1883

1.e4	**e5**
2.Nf3	**Nc6**
3.Bb5	**g6**

Steinitz was also the person who championed this move in answer to 3.Nc3. However, his experiments with 3.Nc3 g6 failed occasionally (e.g. 4.d4 exd4 5.Nd5 and now to avoid 5...Nge7 6.Bg5 he tried 5...Bc5? 6.Bc4 d6 7.Bg5 f6 8.Bh4 Kf8 9.Qd2 Kg7 in Rosenthal-Steinitz, London 1883 - which he lost).

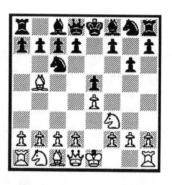

4.d4

From the very first, the strength of this move has always been appreciated. Also in this tournament Simon Winawer tried 4.Bxc6?! against Steinitz (see Chapter One).

4...	**exd4**
5.Nxd4	

But 5.Bg5! went relatively unrecognized for a few years. Today it is seen as the only serious bid for advantage (Chapter Three).

5...	Bg7
6.Be3	Nf6
7.Nc3	O-O
8.O-O	Ne7!

A typically Steinitzian retreat. Black will gain the lost tempo back with 9...c6 and then build a center with 10...d5. The e7-Knight will then be ready to occupy f5 or d5.

9.h3?

In another game from this tournament, Berthold Englisch played 9.Qd2 against Steinitz and turned over the two-Bishop edge after 9...d5 10.exd5 Nexd5 11.Nxd5 Qxd5 12.Be2 Ng4. And in another game, Alexander Sellman, a young master from Baltimore, played 9.Bc4 but also lost his way after 9...d5.

9...	c6
10.Bd3	d5

Black's pawns threaten to corral a piece with 11...c5 and 12...d4.

| 11.exd5 | Nexd5 |

12.Nxd5	Nxd5

And since the e3-Bishop cannot move, White's pawns get messed up and he is left with dark-square weaknesses.

13.c3	Nxe3
14.fxe3	Qg5
15.Qf3	Bd7
16.Bc4	Rae8!

Black invites his opponent into the 17.Bxf7+ Kh8 pin that he cannot get out of (18...Re7).

17.Rae1	Be5
18.Ne2	Re7
19.Nf4	Kg7

Note how–in the absence of an enemy Bishop that operates on dark squares–Black has placed all of his available forces on dark squares.

20.Rd1	Bc8
21.Rf2	Bc7!
22.Kh1	Qe5
23.Re1	

In a bad position, White plays without a plan.

23...	Bf5
24.Kg1	Rfe8
25.g4?	Be4
26.Qd1	Rd8

In fact, he has presented Black with a fine winning plan–the domination of the d-file. First, Black decides to secure the Bishop's position on e4.

27.Qe2	Red7
28.Qf1	Kh8
29.h4	f5!

Now 30.gxf5 Qxf5 would allow the decisive entrance of the Queen.

30.g5	Rd2
31.Qh3	Rxf2
32.Kxf2	Qc5

The threats of 33...Qxc4 and 33...Bxf4 force a won endgame.

33.Ne6	Qxc4
34.Nxd8	Bxd8
35.Qg3	Qd5
36.c4	Qd7

Not falling for 36...Qxc4 37.Qe5+ and 38.Qe8+.

37.Qe5+	Kg8
38.Re2	h6
39.Ke1	Bc7
40.Qd4	Bg3+
41.Kd2	Qxd4+
42.exd4	Bxh4

Facing two passed kingside pawns supported by two Bishops, there was no reason for White to continue the game.

43.gxh6	Bg5+
44.Ke1	Bxh6
45.Kf2	Kf7
46.b3	Bf4
47.a4	g5
48.a5	g4

White resigns

Steinitz had many students and some of them adopted 3...g6 even if the system didn't quite match their style. For example, Harry Nelson Pillsbury, who liked to defend the Lopez with the free-spirited Berlin Defense, also used the fianchetto often in his early career:

Jackson Showalter-Harry Nelson Pillsbury
New York 1893

1.e4	e5
2.Nf3	Nc6
3.Bb5	g6
4.c3	d6
5.d4	Bd7

This makes a rather stodgy impression but it is quite promising in the hands of a positionally skilled player.

6.O-O	Bg7
7.Be3	Nge7
8.Ne1	

For lack of a better idea, White decides to open the f-file with f2-f4.

8...	O-O
9.f4	exd4!
10.cxd4	d5!

This breaks open White's attractive center, as Black can meet 11.e5 with 11...Nxc5! 12.Bxd7 Nxd7.

| 11.Bxc6 | Bxc6 |

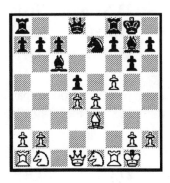

12.f5

White evidently didn't like the looks of 12.e5 Nf5. Black is beginning to gain a clear edge.

| 12... | f6 |
| 13.fxg6 | Nxg6?! |

Although this move is hard to explain and leads to problems with Nd3-f4-h5.

14.Qb3?	**Kh8**
15.Nc3	**Ne7**
16.Rd1	**Qd7**
17.Nd3	**b6**
18.Nf4	**Rad8**
19.Rd2	**Rg8**
20.Nh5?	

Here, however, better was 20.exd5.

20...	**dxe4**
21.d5	**Bxd5**
22.Nxd5	**Nxd5**
23.Nxf6	**Bxf6**
24.Rxf6	**c5**
25.Rff2	**Qe6**

With an extra–and very dangerous–e-pawn Black has good winning chances. White now tries to exploit the c3-h8 diagonal.

26.Rxd5?	**Rxd5**
27.Qc3+	**Qe5**
28.Bd2	

This allows a clever finish.

28...	**e3!**
29.Rf5	**exd2!**

30.Rxe5   **d1=Q+**
31.Re1+   **Qd4+!**
White resigns

But the Fianchetto Defense needed the likes of Pillsbury and Steinitz to keep it popular, and it soon fell out of favor. In the 20th century attempts to revive the Fianchetto Defense were made by Rudolf Spielmann, Akiba Rubinstein and Alexander Alekhine - without much success.

In the last two decades, however, the variation has made a strong comeback. First, in the hands of Vasily Smyslov, Black showed that a number of book positions were not so advantageous to White as theoreticians had claimed.

Then came another major step. Players found that using a slightly different move order –with 3...Nge7 before 4...g6 –Black could avoid some of the most tactically dangerous positions of the 3...g6 Fianchetto Defense. We will consider both move orders - and their many transpositions - in the pages that follow.

Chapter One: The Traditional Fianchetto Defense, 3...g6
Chapter Two: White Meets 3...g6 with 4.c3
Chapter Three: White Meets 3...g6 with 4.d4
Chapter Four: Black's Alternate Route, 3...Nge7
Chapter Five: White's Alternatives at Move 10
Chapter Six: Main Line 3...Nge7

CHAPTER ONE
The Traditional Fianchetto Defense, 3...g6

1.e4	e5
2.Nf3	Nc6
3.Bb5	g6

For some reason, it was in the last two decades of the 19th century that most alternatives to the Morphy Defense (3...a6) got their first serious trials in tournament chess. Some of them, like the Schliemann (3...f5) and Classical (3...Bc5) Defenses came back into fashion periodically in the 20th century. Others, like 3...Qf6 and 3...Bb4 never gained much respectability.

The fate of 3...g6 has yet to be determined but it surely belongs in the first group, rather than the latter.

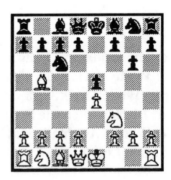

There are only two serious alternatives here to the popular choices of 4.c3 and 4.d4, and we will consider them first. One alternative is the exchange variation, a) 4.Bxc6. The other is the somewhat colorless b) 4.Nc3.

a) 4.Bxc6

4.Bxc6

This doesn't seem to make much sense here since ...Bg7 will solve Black's main problem in similar positions, a solid way of defending the e5-pawn. But the exchange on c6 has been played a few times by some pretty good players–like Emanuel Lasker.

4...   dxc6

As usual, there is no strong reason to justify 4...bxc6. Black now wants to exert as much influence over d4 as he can, thereby preventing White from liberating his Rooks with d2-d4.

5.d3

Of course, as against 3...g6, White cannot win a pawn with 5.Nxe5 because of 5...Qd4, with a liquidation of the center that should be favorable to Black. An odd-looking but reasonable idea here is the counter-fianchetto of 5.b3!?.   A comparable idea is often seen in the Delayed Exchange Variation of the Lopez (1.e4 e5 2.Nf3 Nc6 3.Bb5 a6 4.Ba4 Nf6 5.0-0 Be7 6.Bxc6 dxc6 7.d3 Nd7 8.Nbd2 Bf6?! 9.b3 and 10.Bb2).

After 5.b3 Black should build a center of dark-squared pawns to prevent White's planned d2-d4. For example, 5.b3 Bg7 6.Bb2 and now 6...Qe7 7.d3 c5 8.Nbd2 (Hodges-Pillsbury, New York 1893) leaves Black with problems developing his Knight. Better is 6...Qd6 7.d3 c5 8.Nbd2 Be6 and ...Ne7-c6.

5...	**Bg7**
6.Nc3	**Be6**
7.Be3	

On 7.Bg5 Black should continue 7...Ne7 and if 8.Qd2 c5 9.Bh6, then 9...Bxh6 10.Qxh6 Qd7 followed by ...0-0-0 and ...Nc6-d4.

7...   Qe7

Because White is not exerting much pressure on e5, Black need not post his Queen on d6, where it can be harassed by Knights.

Black stops d2-d4 and prepares the lengthy but rewarding maneuver ...Nf6-d7-b8!-c6-d4. We are following Winawer-Steinitz, London 1883 and Lasker-Pillsbury, New York 1893. Black won the former but lost the latter (due to some awful pawn moves). Regardless of those outcomes, Black stands well here. See Illustrative Game 1 for typical play.

The other somewhat irregular–and unambitious–answers to 3...g6 are 4.Nc3 and 4.d3. We'll consider them here.

b) 4.Nc3

(after 1.e4 e5 2.Nf3 Nc6 3.Bb5 g6)

4.Nc3

The equally quiet 4.d3 should transpose into lines below, unless White adopts a Steinitzian strategy such as 4.d3 Bg7 5.c3 Nge7 6.Nbd2 0-0 and now 7.Nf1!? followed by 8.Ne3, delaying castling. This is a little suspicious here because Black can act in the center with 7...d5 or 7...f5.

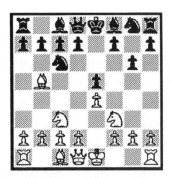

There is a rule of thumb in the Ruy Lopez: when White defends his e4-pawn, he is usually threatening Black's e5-pawn. Here this shouldn't be a problem for Black because he will defend that pawn with...

4...   Bg7

Whenever White plays 4.Nc3 in the irregular Lopez lines–against 3...Bc5, 3...Nge7, 3...f5 and so on–Black has the option of 4...Nd4, since an exchange on d4 eases his game. This Knight advance is available here too but the text is more consistent.

5.d3

In contrast with the comparable 3...Nge7 position (with 4.Nc3 g6) White may offer a gambit here with 5.d4?! but it has very little justification after 5...Nxd4. The text is a quiet prelude to a middlegame in which White will probably continue Be3 (or Bg5) and Qd2 followed, probably, by Bh6 and 0-0-0.

5...   Nge7

Now 6.0-0 lacks ambition and leaves Black with easy equality, e.g. 6...0-0 7.Bd2 Nd4–a common idea in such positions–8.Nxd4 exd4 9.Ne2 d5! 10.exd5 Nxd5 11.Qc1 c5 and Black had no problems in Walbrodt-Pillsbury, Hastings 1895.

6.Bg5

It is worth tickling the enemy kingside with this move, since Black may eventually find it necessary or desirable to play ...f7-f6 or ...h7-h6. On the other hand, 6.h4 may be met by 6...h5 or 6...h6 7.h5 g5.

6...   h6

The best thing about this move is that the Bishop has no ideal retreat. If it goes to e3, it invites ...Nd4 because then Nxd4 and ...exd4 would fork two White pieces.

7.Be3

And if the Bishop retreats to h4 it will be buried by a subsequent ...g6-g5. Then, lacking a way of opening files for his Rooks, White will have a most unpromising middlegame in his future.

7...   Nd4!

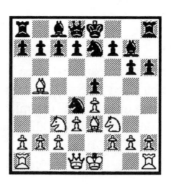

After this Black is playing for more than equality–since he is already equal. Now 8...Nxb5 is a significant threat.

8.Ba4

On this square the Bishop is less vulnerable to ...c7-c6 and ...d7-d5 than on c4. Compare this with 8.Bc4 c6 9.Bxd4 exd4 10.Ne2 after which Rolf Schwarz cites a German game that went 10...Qb6 11.Bb3 0-0 12.Qd2 a5 13.a4 d5 14.0-0 and now 14...dxe4 should have equalized.

| **8...** | **O-O** |
| **9.O-O** | **d6** |

Black can play for ...f7-f5 if he needs a quick open file.

10.Bxd4

This is a major decision but it is hard to suggest a better idea. Clearly, White is not ready to admit that his entire opening is wrong by playing 10.Nb1!?.

| **10...** | **exd4** |
| **11.Ne2** | **Bg4** |

White hoped with his 10th move that the d4-pawn would prove to be a target for him–and an obstruction for Black. However, the idea of 12...Bxf3 or ...f7-f5 ensures that Black has a good position.

Thus far, we have Bertok-Trifunovic, Bled 1961. After 12.Ng3 f5! Black had little difficulty in reaching a good middlegame–and then a good endgame:

13.Bb3+	Kh7
14.h3	Bxf3
15.Qxf3	f4
16.Ne2	Qd7
17.Qg4	Qxg4.

Illustrative Games

1) Winawer-Steinitz, London 1883

1.e4	e5
2.Nf3	Nc6
3.Bb5	g6
4.Bxc6!?	dxc6

Here 4...bxc6 is possible but 5.d4 gives White the better chances.

5.d3	Bg7
6.Be3	Qe7
7.Nc3	Be6
8.O-O	

White apparently was worried about 8.d4 0-0-0!.

8...	h6
9.Nd2	g5!?

Black shuts off the enemy's best chance for opening the game (f2-f4). Now White must consider the risks of playing g2-g3 and f2-f4, or of turning to the queenside with a2-a3 and b2-b4.

10.a3	Nf6
11.f3	Nd7

White was ready for 12.d4. However, Black now begins taking too many time-consuming liberties.

12.Qe2	h5?!
13.Qf2	b6
14.Rfe1	c5
15.Rab1	Nb8

The Knight is headed for d4. If Steinitz did not invent this maneuver he at least is the one who made it famous. But White now sees his chance to act in the center.

16.Nd5!	Bxd5
17.exd5	Nd7
18.c4	f6

19.d4!   cxd4
20.Bxd4

Because of Black's dalliance White stands quite well and can prepare c4-c5.

20...   Qf7
21.Be3   h4
22.Ne4   O-O

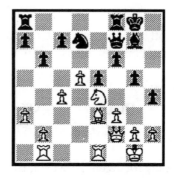

About time! Now White should have gotten an edge with 23.b4 and a general advance of his queenside majority. But here he begins to worry about ...f6-f5—making that move all the more dangerous.

23.g4?!   hxg3
24.hxg3   Qg6
25.Qg2   f5!
26.Nxg5   f4

All of a sudden Black has a dangerous attack, an open Bishop diagonal and a great e5 Knight outpost—at small cost.

27.gxf4   exf4
28.Bf2   Ne5

29.Bh4?	**Rf5**
30.Kf1	

The Knight cannot retreat because of 30...Nxf3+.

30...	**Bf6**
31.Qc2	**Re8**
32.Ne6	**Nxf3!**
33.Bxf6	

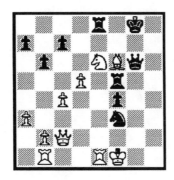

There was little to be done about the various threats of 33...Qg1+, 33...Nxe1, 33...Bxh4 and so on.

33...	**Qg1+**
34.Ke2	**Qe3+**
35.Kf1	**Nd2+**

Now 36.Kg2 Qg3+ leads to mate.

36.Qxd2	**Qxd2**

With a Queen for two minor pieces, Black has an easily won game.

37.Bc3	**Qd3+**

37.Bc3	Qd3+
38.Kf2	Qg3+
39.Ke2	Rh5
40.Kd1	Rh2
41.Kc1	Qf2

White resigns

CHAPTER TWO

White Meets 3...g6 with 4.c3

1.e4	**e5**
2.Nf3	**Nc6**
3.Bb5	**g6**

This move is often used by players who are willing to reach a Steinitz Defense–but prefer this move order. For example, Gata Kamsky, since he was a junior star in the Soviet Union, has used the move order 3...g6 4.c3 d6 and then 5.0-0 Bg7 6.d4 Bd7 7.Re1 Nf6. With the moves ...a7-a6 and Ba4 inserted, this position has occurred often in the Steinitz Defense Deferred.

4.c3

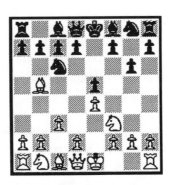

This is the natural response to Black's fianchetto: White hopes to build a center with d2-d4 that will stifle the g7-Bishop. And it is regarded as a good plan. In fact, after this move, virtually all opening authorities give Black two choices: he can play 4...d6 or put the eternal question to the Bishop with 4...a6 first. In the latter case, Black's move order appears very suspicious because 4...a6 offers White the promising retreat to c4, rather than to a4. However, Black's choices are not that limited.

4...   Bg7

Modern Chess Openings, 13th Edition says simply that this is a dubious move because after 5.d4 Black must give up the center. Similar comments are found in other opening manuals. There is, incidentally, another way for Black to play this. He can reply with 4...Qe7 and then 5.d4 Nf6, counterattacking in the center as in the Giuoco Piano. This idea, however, has not seen serious testing.

5.d4

Note that 5.0-0 Nge7 would transpose into Chapter Five. The best White achieves in those lines is a very small edge, so here 5.d4 must be considered a more critical challenge.

5...   Nge7

And here, too, 6.0-0 exd4 would transpose into Chapter Five. It should be noted, however, that Black can continue in the same vein as our main line below by meeting 6.0-0 with 6...0-0!? and then 7.d5 a6!. For example, 8.Be2 Na7 9.d6 cxd6 10.Qxd6 Nb5 11.Bxb5 axb5 12.Rd1 Ra6!? as in Kurajica-Palacios, Montilla 1972.

If White declines to push his pawn to d6, Black should have an easier time: 9.c4 d6 10.Nc3 c6 and now Dobrovolsky-Zolnierowicz, Karvina 1989 went 11.a4? a5 12.Qb3 c5 13.Bd2 h6 14.Ne1 f5 with advantage to Black. His kingside attack is rolling but White has shot himself in the foot on the queenside.

6.d5

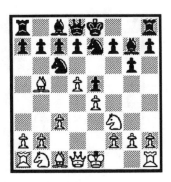

6...   a6!

Not just putting the question to the Bishop - this move also creates a flight square for the Knight at a7. And not a bad flight square at that, as we'll see.

Here White has a choice of retreats, chiefly between a) 7.Ba4 and b) 7.Be2. An immediate capture (7.dxc6 axb5 8.cxd7+ Bxd7 or 7.Bxc6 dxc6!) must help Black.

a) 7.Ba4

7.Ba4

This keeps control of a good diagonal (a4-e8) but the Bishop may remain out of play, particularly after ...Nb5.

7...   Na7

Not 7...Nb8 because 8.d6 cxd6 9.Qxd6 leaves Black's development paralyzed.

8.d6

This is the crucial test of Black's play. Alternatives such as 8.c4 0-0 9.Nc3 d6 are unconvincing. Such positions usually pit White's queenside initiative (c4-c5) against Black's kingside chances (...f7-f5). Black's Knight would then be misplaced on a7, but so would White's Bishop on a4.

8...	cxd6
9.Qxd6	Nb5

This is the point of Black's play since move six. Now 10.Bxb5 axb5 11.0-0 0-0 would likely transpose into the main line below or to section b).

10.Qd3

The Queen is well placed here and threatens to win a pawn.

10...	O-O!?

A recurring theme in the Fianchetto Defense is Black's willingness to sacrifice a pawn to complete development and obtain the two Bishops.

11.Bxb5	axb5
12.O-O	

Grabbing the pawn immediately also makes sense. After 12.Qxb5 d5 13.exd5 Nxd5 14.0-0 e4 or 12.Nbd2 dxe4 13.Nxe4 Bf5 14.Ng3 Bd3 Black has play but White has a pawn.

12...   d5

A complex middlegame is about to begin, with Black's queenside a mess - yet his center is promising. The best test of this line so far appears to be Kudrin-Sanz, Salamanca 1989, which went 13.Rd1 f5 14.Qxb5 fxe4 15.Nfd2 Bg4 16.Re1 Qd6 after which Black was not worse.

b) 7.Be2

(after 1.e4 e5 2.Nf3 Nc6 3.Bb5 g6 4.c3 Bg7 5.d4 Nge7 6.d5 a6)

7.Be2

The Bishop has more of a future on this square than on a4. Note that on d3 the Bishop would deny White's Queen access to d6, thereby making 8.d6 a more dubious idea.

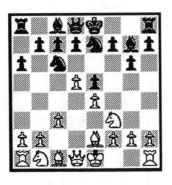

7...   Na7
8.d6

Again, a natural move. But 8.c4 may be better now that the Bishop is on e2 rather than a4. After 8...d6 9.Nc3 0-0 Boris Spassky has tried 10.h4, so as to meet 10...f5 with 11.h5. A game Spassky-Sanz, Montilla-Morilles 1978 went 11...f4 12.Bd2 h6 13.hxg6 Nxg6 14.Qb3 with superior chances. Black may do better with 9...c5 (instead of 9...0-0) and then 10.h4 h5 or 10.0-0 0-0 11.Rb1? b5!.

8...	cxd6
9.Qxd6	Nb5

This move is essential is Black is to avoid disadvantage. Now 10.Qd3 as in a) above is poor because White cannot even capture on b5 then.

10.Bxb5	axb5
11.Na3	

Again, 11.0-0 looks best, after which 11...0-0 12.Rd1 Ra6 is one attractive line.

11...	Ra6
12.Qd3	

Note that 12.Nxb5? Rxd6 13.Nxd6+ Kf8 is quite unsound: 14.Ng5 f6 15.Ngf7 Qc7 and Black consolidates his material edge.

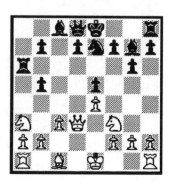

12...	b4!

A strong move that is based on 13.cxb4 d5 with excellent prospects for Black. If White, instead, plays 13.Nc2, Black captures on c3 and pushes his d-pawn (13...bxc3 14.bxc3 d5 15.Ba3 0-0). For the third move, 13.Nb5, see Illustrative Game 2.

Illustrative Game

2) Gola-Zolnierowicz
Karvina 1989

1.e4	e5
2.Nf3	Nc6
3.Bb5	g6
4.c3	Bg7
5.d4	Nge7
6.d5	

This move is regarded as punishing Black's play in most books that cover 3...g6.

6...	**a6**
7.Be2	**Na7**
8.d6	**cxd6**
9.Qxd6	**Nb5**
10.Bxb5	**axb5**
11.Na3	**Ra6**
12.Qd3	**b4**

And here 13.Nc4 d5 14.Ncxe5 f6! would end the game quickly. Better is 14.exd5 Nxd5 with relatively equal chances.

13.Nb5	**O-O**

Or just 13...d5 as Black plays against other moves by the c3 Knight. Now White gets a chance to slow the d-pawn with 14.c4.

14.cxb4	**d5**
15.O-O?	**f5**

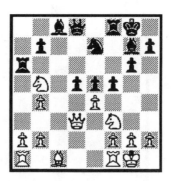

Black has a wonderful center and bright middlegame prospects.

16.exd5	**e4**

17.Qb3!

Otherwise he loses a piece. Now 17...exf3 18.d6+ favors White.

17...	Qxd5
18.Nfd4	Qxb3

But the endgame also favors him thanks to superior pawns and the weak White queenside.

19.Nxb3	Nd5
20.a3	Bd7
21.N5d4	Rd6?

This gives White new hope. After 21...Ba4! Black is on the road to winning.

22.Bd2	Ba4
23.Nc5!	Bxd4
24.Nxa4	f4
25.Bc3	Ba7

Now with 26.Nc5, blocking the dangerous a7-g1 diagonal, the chances are double-edged.

26.Rad1?	e3!
27.fxe3	fxe3
28.Nc5	Nf4!

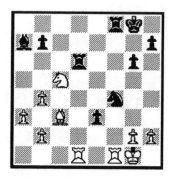

Threatening, among other things, 29...e2. Note that 29.Rxd6 allows mate in two (29...Ne2+).

29.Rfe1?	Rxd1
30.Rxd1	Ne2+
31.Kh1	Nxc3
32.bxc3	e2

The pawn now queens. White plays it out to the bitterest end.

33.Rg1	Rf1
34.Nd3	Rxg1 mate

CHAPTER THREE

White Meets 3...g6 with 4.d4

By far the most dangerous test of 3...g6, according to a host of opening authorities, is the dynamic break in the center at move four.

1.e4	**e5**
2.Nf3	**Nc6**
3.Bb5	**g6**
4.d4	

In a comparable reversed position from the Vienna Game (1.e4 e5 2.Nc3 Nf6 3.g3), the recommended move for Black is 3...d5. With the extra move (Bb5) White should have good chances here. But it is not clear that Bb5 fits in well with d2-d4 before Black has played ...d7-d6.

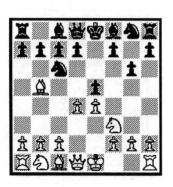

4...	**exd4**

The old books recommended 4...Nxd4 (to avoid 4...exd4 5.Bg5). However, the Knight capture leads to a somewhat questionable position after 5.Nxd4 exd4 6.Qxd4 Qf6 7.e5.

The exchange of pawns on d4 is actually quite good for Black in a positional sense. His g7-Bishop obtains a longer diagonal and Black also gets a half-open e-file with which to attack White's remaining pawn in the center. But what is good positionally is often bad tactically. If White now plays 5.Nxd4, there is no serious tactical problem and Black should equalize - at least. The tactical problem arises after 5.Bg5!, considered in section b) later in this chapter. Black's natural response, 5...Be7, also leads to a White choice and we'll consider those options at the appropriate moment.

a) 5.Nxd4

5.Nxd4

This doesn't trouble Black's development in the least.

5...   Bg7

The first real threat in the game. The position now resembles an Accelerated Dragon Sicilian (1.e4 c5 2.Nf3 Nc6 3.d4 cxd4 4.Nxd4 g6) with the primary difference being that it is Black's e-pawn, not the c-pawn, that has been exchanged off here. White can meet the threat to his d4-Knight by capturing 6.Nxc6. But 6...dxc6 leads to a balanced endgame according to Siegbert Tarrasch in the book of the great Hastings 1895 tournament. In that event, Pillsbury preferred to stay in the middlegame with 6...bxc6 and obtained a solid game after 7.Bc4 Ne7 8.Nc3 d6 9.0-0 Be6 10.Bb3 0-0 11.Be3 c5!.

6.Bxc6?!

A common theme in Lopez variations is to give up this Bishop on c6 in order to preserve a Knight on d4. After the more natural 6.Be3 we head into positions that occurred often a century ago but have long since been discovered to be painless for Black. After 6...Nge7 we transpose into Chapter Four but 6...Nf6, as played by Steinitz, looks better. Then 7.Nc3 0-0 and 8...Ne7! prepares a ...d7-d5 punch that should at least equalize. See Illustrative Game 3.

6...   dxc6!

Renews the attack on d4.

7.c3

Not 7.Be3 because of 7...c5 and 8...Bxb2.

7...   c5!

This offers the prospect of an exchange of Queen's that assures Black of a small initiative–and at least equality.

8.Nb3

After 8.Nb5 Bd7 and ...Bc6 Black also stands well.

8...   Qxd1+

9.Kxd1   b6

This last move not only protects the c5-pawn but opens up the a8-e4 diagonal for the c8-Bishop.

10.Bg5

It is hard to find a better plan for White. He has a kingside majority but Black's superior development should prevent that from becoming a factor.

10...   f6
11.Bf4   Bb7

Now 12.Bxc7 Kd7 13.Bg3 Bxe4 is a good, indirect exchange of pawns.

12.f3   O-O-O+

And Black had a perfectly even position in Hansen-Rantanen, Gausdal 1987. Since the discovery of a better fifth move by White hardly anyone ventures 5.Nxd4 any more.

We should, therefore, focus our attention on the greatest challenge to 3...g6:

b) 5.Bg5

(after 1.e4 e5 2.Nf3 Nc6 3.Bb5 g6 4.d4 exd4)

5.Bg5!

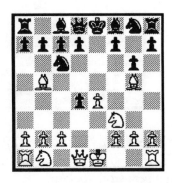

This simple threat to the Queen is dangerous because whatever Black does in response weakens his position. If he plays 5...f6 he ruins his pawn structure and blocks the g7-d4 line. If he retreats the c6-Knight to e7 he allows 6.Qxd4. And 5...Nge7? 6.Bf6 is too horrible to consider seriously.

5...   .   Be7

Here we must diverge a bit further, considering three responses by White: b1) the retreat 6.Bf4, and b2) the "attacking" 6.h4, and b3) the natural 6.Bxe7.

b1) The Retreat 6.Bf4

6.Bf4

This recommendation of Paul Keres' loses a bit of time. But White reasons that he'll get the tempo back when Black tries to sort out the misplacement of the e7-Bishop.

6...   Nf6

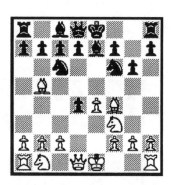

This is much better than trying to correct the Bishop's problems with 6...Bf6. Since White's sixth move is a tempo-losing finesse, Black wants to make a lead in development work for him.

7.e5

The gambit of the e-pawn (7.0-0) appears unsound after 7...a6 8.Ba4 Nxe4 9.Re1 Nc5! 10.Bxc6 dxc6 as in Wellendorf-Dautov, Baden-Baden 1990.

7...   Nd5

Clearly better than 7...Nh5 8.Bh6.

8.Bh6

Perhaps best now is 8...a6 since 9.Ba4 Nb6 10.Bb3 d5! appears to favor Black and 9.Bc4 Nb6 10.Bb3 transposes.

Also, 9.Bxc6 dxc6 10.Qxd4 Nb4! may be just as good for Black in the resulting endgame. See Illustrative Game 4.

8...   Bb4+!?

This strange move delays White's recapture on d4. The immediate 8...Bf8 9.Bxf8 Kxf8 10.Nxd4 appears to favor White slightly.

9.Nbd2   Bf8!
10.Bxf8

No better is 10.Bg5 Be7, repeating the position.

10...   Kxf8
11.Nc4

White plays to regain the pawn immediately. No better is 11.0-0 d6 12.Bxc6 bxc6 13.exd6 c5!, preserving the strong pawn at d4. Then 14.Ne4 cxd6 15.Nxd4 Qe7 is equal (Levchenkov-Kirillov, Riga 1986).

11...   Qe7

Threatening the big check at b4, winning a piece.

12.O-O

Now 12.Bxc6 bxc6!? and 13...Ba6 is easy for Black to play.

12...   Qb4
13.Bxc6   (see next diagram)
13...   Qxc4!

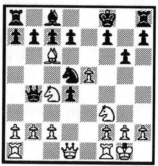

After 13.Bxc6

This may equalize according to Yuri Averbach (14.Bxd5 Qxd5 followed by ...Kg7, ...d7-d6, and ...Re8).

b2) The Attacking 6.h4

(after 1.e4 e5 2.Nf3 Nc6 3.Bb5 g6 4.d4 exd4 5.Bg5 Be7)

6.h4

This is the only move that allows the Bishop to remain on g5. The h-pawn can later be advanced to open up Black's castled position.

6...	**Nf6!**

Again, this useful attack on e4 leads to equality. On the other hand, 6...h6?! 7.Bf4! only helps the enemy out by creating a favorable version of a).

7.e5

After 7.Nbd2 Black can safely castle with good chances (7...0-0 8.Qe2 d5).

7...   Ng4

Now White's e5-pawn is as much of a target as Black's d4-pawn. White's best policy is not clear at this point but 8.Bf4 f6 and 8.Qe2 0-0 do not appear convincing. Let's now consider the main line of 5.Bg5:

b3) The Natural 6.Bxe7

(after 1.e4 e5 2.Nf3 Nc6 3.Bb5 g6 4.d4 exd4 5.Bg5 Be7)

6.Bxe7

This is the common sense approach and has been the most successful in practice. White hopes to exploit the holes on f6 and h6 now that the Bishop that would guard those squares is off the board.

6...   Ngxe7

There is something to be said about 6...Qxe7 but Black here does not intend to develop the Knight more aggressively on f6. Rather, he wants to make sure he can play ...d7-d5.

7.Nxd4

For years 3...g6 had a bad reputation - primarily because of games that continued 7...0-0 8.Nc3 a6? 9.Nxc6 bxc6 10.Bd3 with a slight edge for White.

7...   d5

This leads into an even endgame. More adventurous spirits will prefer 7...0-0 8.Nc3 d5. Then 9.0-0 dxe4 10.Bxc6 Nxc6 11.Nxc6 bxc6 12.Nxe4 Bf5 is just as equal as the endgame mentioned in the next note - but with Queens still on the board.

White may try for more with 9.exd5 Nxd5 10.Nxc6, but 10...Qe8+ 11.Qe2 bxc6 also holds the balance. Similarly, 10.Bxc6 Nxc3! 11.bxc3 bxc6 12.0-0 Qf6 (Romero Holmes-Vladimirov, Leon 1991).

8.Nc3

8...   0-0!

Transposing into the above note. This is more promising than 8...dxe4 9.Bxc6+ Nxc6 10.Nxc6 Qxd1+ 11.Rxd1 bxc6 12.Nxe4 Bf5 after which 13.Rd4! O-O 14.Ng3 appears to give White the upper hand: 14...Bxc2 15.Kd2 Bf5 16.Nxf5 gxf5 17.Rc1 with a clear edge. Now 9.O-O dxe4 should lead to equality, as noted above.

Illustrative Games

3) Teichmann-Pillsbury
Hastings 1895

1.e4	e5
2.Nf3	Nc6
3.Bb5	g6
4.d4	exd4
5.Nxd4	Bg7
6.Be3	Nf6

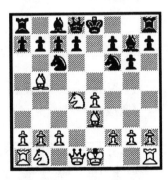

This move puts more pressure on the center than 6...Nge7 and also keeps e7 free for the other Knight.

7.Nc3	O-O
8.f3?	

This move is perfectly reasonable in a Dragon Variation of the Sicilian—but quite wrong here. Perhaps 8.Nxc6 dxc6 9.Be2 is best, but that's not saying much.

8...   Ne7!
9.O-O

To show how the same mistakes are played over and over, the same 8.f3? Ne7 occurred 96 years later in the game Duckstein-Smyslov, Bad Worishofen 1991. White tried to exert more control on d5 with 9.Nde2 but 9...d5! 10.exd5 Nfxd5 still gave Black an advantage.

There followed 11.Bg5 c6 12.Nxd5 cxd5 13.c3 Qd6 14.Qd2 Nc6 and then 15.Rd1 Be6 16.Nd4 Nxd4! 17.cxd4 Rfc8 was eventually converted by Black into a decisive use of the c-file.

9...   c6
10.Bd3   d5

Pillsbury was well aware of the games of his mentor, Steinitz. Now 11.e5 Ne8 and 12...c5 would be dangerous for White.

11.Nde2   dxe4
12.fxe4   Ng4

This is White's problem in so many Sicilians. The attacked Bishop cannot leave the g1-d4 diagonal because of 13...Qb6+.

13.Qd2	**Qd6!**

Better than the immediate 13...Nxe3 because Black can derive one additional benefit from the Knight being on g4.

14.g3	**Qe5**
15.Rae1	**Nxe3**
16.Qxe3	**Nf5**
17.Qf3	**Nd4!**

This assures Black control of d4 and other key dark squares.

18.Nxd4	**Qxd4+**
19.Kg2	**Qb4!**
20.e5	**Qxb2**

This is enough to decide the game, so White throws himself into a desperate attack against f7.

21.Bc4	**Qxc2+**
22.Rf2	**Qf5!**

| 23.Qe3 | Qh3+ |
| 24.Kg1 | Be6 |

And the attack is over almost before it began. White has one last trap.

25.Be2	Qh6
26.Rf4	Qg5
27.Bd3	Rad8
28.Qf3?	Bxe5!
29.h4	Bd4+

Based on 30.Rxd4 Qc5 and Black remains three pawns ahead.

| 30.Kh2 | Qa5 |
| **White resigns** | |

4) Timoshchenko-Kholmov
Moscow 1988

1.e4	e5
2.Nf3	Nc6
3.Bb5	g6
4.d4	exd4
5.Bg5	Be7
6.Bf4	Nf6

It's useful for Black to hit the e4-pawn before White can defend it with Nc3.

7.e5	Nd5
8.Bh6	a6
9.Bxc6	

Regains the pawn but at the cost of entering a dubious endgame. As noted earlier, 9.Bc4 or 9.Ba4 are met by 9...Nb6 10.Bb3 d5!.

9...	dxc6
10.Qxd4	Nb4!
11.Qxd8+	

The trade is forced because of the vulnerability of c2, e.g. 11.Qe4 Bf5 or 11.Qc3 Bf5 12.Nd4? Qxd4!.

11...	Bxd8
12.Kd2!?	Bg4!
13.Nc3	Bxf3
14.gxf3	Bh4

Black keeps the initiative by tieing his opponent to the defense of f2.

15.Raf1	f5

16.a3	O-O-O+
17.Kc1	Nd5
18.Ne2	Rhe8

White has a protected passed pawn but a bad Bishop and clumsy Rooks.

19.f4	Rd7
20.Ng1!	

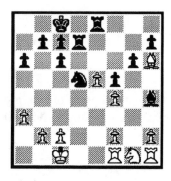

This kicks the h4-Bishop back and frees White's kingside pieces.

20...	c5
21.Nf3	Be7
22.Ng1	c4
23.c3	

If Black is allowed to undouble his pawns by 23...c3 he would have a significant edge. Now Black finds a way to maneuver his Knight to the newly created hole at d3.

23...	Nb6!?
24.h4	Na4

25.Nf3	Nc5
26.Kc2	Nd3
27.h5	Bc5

White now decides against the passive defense of Rh2 and makes a pawn sacrifice.

28.hxg6	hxg6
29.Nd4!?	Bxd4
30.cxd4	Rxd4
31.Rh4	b5
32.Bg5	

With no obvious targets to hit, White waits for the enemy queenside pawns to advance.

32...	Kb7
33.f3	Re6
34.Kc3	c5
35.Kc2	a5
36.Rfh1	Kc6

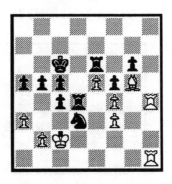

And although White's Rooks now have targets, Black is close to winning.

37.Rh8	b4
38.Rc8+	Kb7
39.Rhh8	b3+
40.Kb1	Nxe5?

An apparent oversight: Black must not have seen the g5-Bishop getting back into the game.

41.fxe5	Rd1+
42.Bc1!	Rxe5
43.Rce8	

This stops 43...Ree1 and preserves the extra piece.

43...	Rxe8
44.Rxe8	a4
45.Re7+	Kc6
46.Re6+	Kb5
47.Rxg6	c3!
48.bxc3	Kc4!

A good try by Black. Now 49.Kb2 Rf1 50.f4 Rf2+ only helps Black.

49.Rc6	**Rd3**
50.f4	**Rxc3**
51.Ra6	**Kb5**
52.Ra5+!	

Forces a draw, since without Rooks on the board the White Bishop easily blockades the pawns.

52...	**Kxa5**
53.Bd2	**Kb5**
54.Bxc3	**Kc4**
55.Kb2	**Kd3**
56.Bf6	**Draw**

CHAPTER FOUR

Black's Alternate Route, 3...Nge7

Because of the tactical problems presented by 4.c3 (Chapter Two) and 4.d4 exd4 5.Bg5 (Chapter Three), many strong players who like to play the Fianchetto Defense have adopted a different move order. The improved version is:

1.e4	**e5**
2.Nf3	**Nc6**
3.Bb5	**Nge7**

Black will continue with 4...g6 and 5...Bg7 if allowed. The combination of 3...Nge7 with the fianchetto has been played for decades but hardly ever given the respect it deserves. For example, in his 318-page book on the Lopez, A.S. Suetin mentioned this move in a kind of footnote, adding that "in our time" (1982!) the move is almost never played. And in Informant No. 15 the Knight move is simply given a question mark–without further comment.

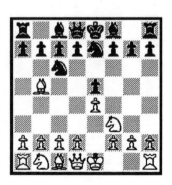

Before we get into the main line of the "Improved Fianchetto" we'll consider the other options available at White's fourth move. He has a choice between four reasonable alternatives: a) 4.d4, b) 4.c3, c) 4.0-0 and d) 4.Nc3.

a) 4.d4

4.d4

This was the most dynamic way of meeting 3...g6, so it seems like a natural way for White to respond to 3...Nge7.

4...   exd4
5.Nxd4

But here's the basic difference: Unlike the comparable 3...g6 position, here 5.Bg5 has no meaning. As a result, Black obtains a good positional middlegame now without risk.

5...   g6

Now 6.0-0 transposes into c) below. If White anticipates 6...Bg7 here by playing 6.Nxc6, Black can retake with a piece and preserve his pawn structure.

And 6.Nxc6 Nxc6 7.Bxc6 can be met by either recapture–but 7...bxc6 is the more aggressive. Then after 7...bxc6 8.Qd4 f6 9.Nc3 Bg7 10.Bf4 d6 11.h4 h5 12.0-0-0 White's position is freer but in S.Polgar-Lazich, Dortmund 1990 Black got the upper hand and won after 12...Be6 13.Qe3 Qb8! 14.f3 Qb6 15.Rdg1 Rb8 16.b3 Qa5.

6.Nc3

Again, it makes sense for White to defend the d4-Knight with his Bishop on e3, as in the line that follows. Note how clumsy 6.Bg5 Bg7 7.c3 looks. For 6.0-0, see section c) below. See also Illustrative Game 5.

6...	Bg7
7.Be3	O-O
8.Qd2	

On 8.0-0 Black can obtain excellent play with 8...d5, as we'll see in c). The text prepares for queenside castling.

| 8... | d5! |

This avoids a passive center position, although 8...d6 and 9...f5 is also possible.

9.O-O-O

On 9.exd5 Black can retake on d5 as a gambit: 9...Nxd5 10.Bxc6 Nxc3! 11.bxc3 bxc6 12.Nxc6 Qf6 or 11.Qxc3 bxc6 12.Qxc6 Bxd4 13.Qxa8 Bxb2 (threatening 14...Bc3+ 15.Kf1 Ba6+ and 16...Qxa8). Similarly, 9.Nxc6 bxc6 10.Bxc6 invites 10...Nxe3 11.Qxe3 Rb8 or 11.Bxa8 Qxd2+ 12.Kxd2 Nc4+ with a dangerous attack.

9...	**dxe4**
10.Nxe4	**Nxd4**

And Black will be fully equal in the endgame that follows 11.Bxd4 Qxd4 12.Qxd4 Bxd4 13.Rxd4 Bf5. Since 4.d4 leads to nothing for White, let's move on to the other move that troubles 3...g6:

b) 4.c3

(after 1.e4 e5 2.Nf3 Nc6 3.Bb5 Nge7)

4.c3

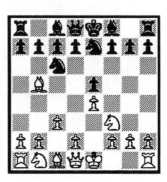

White declares his intention with this move to build a broad pawn center.

4...   **g6**

If Black plays 4...d5, as in a similar position of the Ponziani Opening, White answers with 5.Qe2!.

5.d4   **exd4**
6.cxd4   **d5**

Now with 7.exd5 Nxd5 8.0-0 Bg7 we transpose into our main line, which deserves a fuller treatment. See the next two chapters.

c) 4.0-0

(after 1.e4 e5 2.Nf3 Nc6 3.Bb5 Nge7)

4.O-O

Castling can never be a bad move in the Lopez and it is flexible enough here to meet the demands of the position. White wants to know what Black is planning–4...Ng6 or 4...g6.

4...   **g6**

Now 5.c3 Bg7 6.d4 exd4 7.cxd4 d5 leads directly into the next chapter. White has a more energetic plan here–but it is one that Steinitz discredited back in the 1880's.

5.d4   exd4

Here the gambit idea 6.c3 has been played on rare occasions. Black can probably keep the pawn safely with 6...dxc3 7.Nxc3 Bg7 and if 8.Bg5 then 8...f6!?. But Black also gets a good game–and without risk–by rejecting the pawn with that all-purpose means of declining gambits, 6...d3.

6.Nxd4

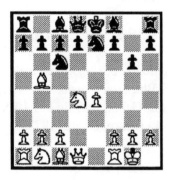

A line reminiscent of Chapter Three (3...g6 4.d4 exd4 5.Bg5) is initiated by 6.Bg5!? here. But in the current position the Bishop move lacks bite and after 6...Bg7 7.c3 Black can just kick the piece with 7...h6. In Romanishin-Smyslov, Moscow 1981, Black had few difficulties after 8.Bd2 d5! 9.Nxd4 dxe4 10.Qa4 0-0.

6...   Bg7

Now 7.c3 0-0 is a position considered favorable to White by some opening texts circa 1893. Of course, today we can see that Black can equalize with a timely ...d7-d5.

7.Be3

Another way of dealing with the attack on d4 is 7.Nxc6. But this reduces tension in the center and should present Black with few middlegame difficulties (7...bxc6 8.Ba4 0-0 9.Nc3 Kh8 10.Be3 d6 11.Bd4 f6 12.Ne2 c5 as in Petersen- Wedberg, Copenhagen 1984).

7...	O-O
8.Nc3	

This resembles the Mackenzie-Steinitz game from the introduction, except that Black's Knights are at c6 and e7, not c6 and f6. Black can now offer a promising gambit with:

8...	d5!?

The solid method is 8...d6, which leads to a somewhat cramped game after 9.Qd2 Ne5. Black stands well, however, after 9.f3 f5 10.Be2 fxe4 11.Nxe4 Nf5 (A. and E. Geller) or 9.Be2 f5 10.Nxc6 Nxc6 11.exf5 Bxf5 with equality in Kolbak- Larsen, Grenaa 1973.

9.exd5	Nxd5

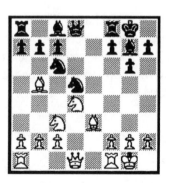

As we saw in section a), in which White had played Qd2 instead of castling, Black has good compensation. Now 10.Bxc6 can be met by 10...Nxc3.

10.Nxc6 bxc6
11.Bxc6

Declining the offer with 11.Nxd5 cxb5! appears preferable, although Black's two Bishops cannot be dismissed. After 12.Bc5 Re8 13.Ne7+ Kh8 he stands well (see Illustrative Game 6).

11... Nxe3!

And now 12.Qxd8 Rxd8 13.Bxa8 Nxf1 is nothing for White (14.Kxf1 Ba6+).

12.fxe3 Rb8

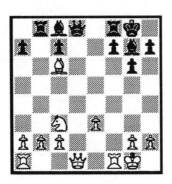

Black has full compensation for his sacrificed pawn in view of the targets at e3 and b2. We are following Kuznetzov-Vul, Protvino 1985 which led to a sharp battle with 13.Bd5 Ba6 14.Rf3 Rxb2 15.Rxf7 Kh8! 16.Ne4 Rxf7 17.Bxf7 Qe7.

Black eventually won after 18.Bb3 h5! 19.Nf2 Qxe3 20.Qd8+ Kh7 21.Qxc7 Kh6 22.Qd6 Rxb3!.

There is one other important option at White's disposal on his fourth turn:

d) 4.Nc3

(after 1.e4 e5 2.Nf3 Nc6 3.Bb5 Nge7)

4.Nc3

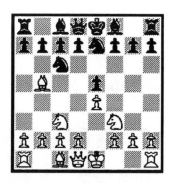

This is the move recommended by Suetin, who suggested that Black should now play 4...Ng6 and if 5.d4 exd4 6.Nxd4, then 6...Bc5.

4...   g6

Quite reasonable alternatives here are 4...Nd4 and 4...Ng6. The text brings matters back into the Fianchetto Defense.

5.d4   exd4

Remarkably, both Suetin and Paul Keres (in the first edition of ECO) gave Black's best line as 5...Bg7 6.Bg5 h6 7.Be3 exd4, after which 8.Nxd4

0-0 9.Qd2 and queenside castling favors White. Suetin did not even mention 5...exd4 in his extensive 1982 work on the Lopez.

6.Nd5

This is the main point of White's fourth move. He threatens mate in one and prepares a damaging 7.Bf4 or 7.Bg5.

6...   Bg7

Here we come to a parting of the ways. White has two attractive moves with his c1-Bishop. He must choose between them or surrender the initiative and begin thinking about regaining his pawn.

The choice is between d1) 7.Bf4 and d2) 7.Bg5.

d1) 7.Bf4

7.Bf4

This looks natural because of the threat to c7 and the trap in the next note. But 7.Bg5 is most likely the better move.

7...   Nxd5!

Not 7...d6? because of the surprise move 8.Bg5! after which the multiple pins must cost Black some material.

8.exd5   Ne7!

Once again Black can allow the enemy to advance a pawn to d6.

9.d6   cxd6
10.O-O   O-O

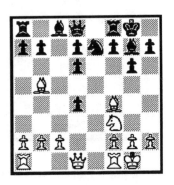

11.Bxd6   Re8

At first glance this position seems fine for White. However, opinions were changed by Zaitsev-Dreev, Moscow 1989, which turned sharply in Black's favor. See Illustrative Game 7. In the absence of any obvious improvements of White's play, attention has turned to a different idea at move seven:

d2) 7.Bg5

(after 1.e4 e5 2.Nf3 Nc6 3.Bb5 Nge7 4.Nc3 g6 5.d4 exd4 6.Nd5 Bg7)

7.Bg5

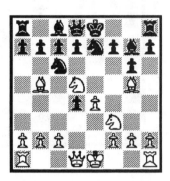

The deficiencies of 7.Bf4 have become evident in recent years but 7.Bg5 remains controversial.

7...   h6

Black cannot allow 8.Bxc6. Now, 7...h6 8.Bxc6 hxg5 only helps Black.

8.Bf6

This looks stronger than it really is.

8...   Bxf6!
9.Nxf6+   Kf8

Black will regain a tempo, and establish a secure kingside, with ...Kg7. He may also play ...Nf5, discovering an attack on the f6-Knight.

10.Nxd4

Better may be 10.0-0 Kg7 11.Nd5, and then 11...Re8 12.Re1 d6 13.Qd2 a6 14.Bxc6 Nxc6 15.Nxd4 favors White slightly (Lanka-Banas, Trnava 1987).

10...   Nf5!

This is better than 10...Kg7 because, instead of 11.Nd5 Nxd5 12.exd5 Re8+ White can play 11.Qd2! Kxf6? 12.Qc3! with a winning attack.

11.exf5

White can make a desperado out of the Knight with 11.Nh7+ Rxh7 12.exf5 thereby putting the Rook offsides. But 12...Qf6 13.fxg6 fxg6 and ...Re7+ or 13.Bxc6 dxc6 14.fxg6 fxg6 15.0-0 Rd7! (Chernov-Vul, Moscow 1992) are perfectly sound for Black.

11...	**Qxf6**
12.Bxc6	**dxc6**
13.fxg6	

13...   Kg7!

Improving over Nadanian-Vul, Moscow 1992 which favored White after 13...fxg6 14.0-0. Now 14.gxf7 Rd8 should equalize without much difficulty.

Illustrative Games

5) Grigoriev-Alekhine,
First Soviet Championship 1920

1.e4	e5
2.Nf3	Nc6
3.Bb5	Nge7
4.d4	exd4
5.Nxd4	g6
6.Bg5?!	Bg7

7.c3

Of course, not 7.Nb3 Bxb2. White's center is now vulnerable to harassment because he can't play a Knight to c3.

7...	h6!

Black needs to retain the option of driving the Bishop off the h4-e°
diagonal.

8.Bh4	O-O
9.O-O	Nxd4!?
10.cxd4	c6

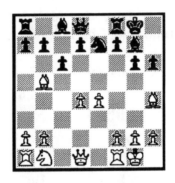

11.Bc4	g5
12.Bg3	d5!

This effectively isolates the d4-pawn.

13.exd5	Nxd5
14.Be5!	Be6
15.Nd2	

It was probably time to get rid of the e5-Bishop with 15.Bxg7.

15...	f6
16.Bg3	Qb6
17.Re1	Rfe8

Now 18.Nf3 Rad8 begins to doom the isolated d-pawn. White plays more aggressively.

18.Ne4	**f5!**
19.Nc5	**Bf7**
20.Bd6	**Qxb2!**

Black wins a pawn, willingly allowing an enemy Rook to penetrate to b7. Now 21.Nb3 is too discouraging, so...

21.Rb1?	**Qxd4**
22.Bxd5	**Bxd5**
23.Rxb7	**Qg4!**

This is what White overlooked: his first rank is susceptible to invasion (24.Qxg4 Rxe1 mate or 24.Rxe8+ Rxe8 25.Qxg4 Re1 mate). And since 24.g3 Qh3 is quite lost, White played two more moves before conceding.

24.f3	**Bd4+!**
25.Kh1	**Bxf3!**
White resigns	

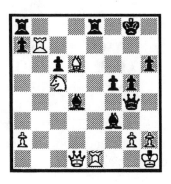

It's mate after 26.Rxe8+ Rxe8 27.gxf3 Re1+! 28.Qxe1 Qxf3.

6) Tiviakov-Shcherbakov
Odessa 1989

1.e4	e5
2.Nf3	Nc6
3.Bb5	Nge7
4.O-O	

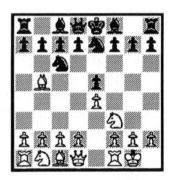

Castling is the move most often chosen by players unfamiliar with Black's third move.

4...	g6
5.d4	exd4
6.Nxd4	Bg7
7.Be3	O-O
8.Nc3	d5!

The bottom line is this: if Black can successfully liquidate the center this way, then the primary difference between the two sides is that Black's king Bishop is better placed than White's.

9.exd5	Nxd5
10.Nxc6	bxc6
11.Nxd5!?	cxb5!

Black gets the two Bishops and White gets a slight initiative now.

12.Bc5	Re8
13.Ne7+	Kh8!
14.Qf3	Be6
15.Rad1	Qb8
16.Nc6	Qb7

But here the mini-initiative is over and White's queenside pawns can become vulnerable.

17.Bd4!	b4
18.Bxg7+	Kxg7
19.b3	h5
20.h3	a5!
21.Rfe1	Ra6

This forces an endgame that cannot be bad for the Bishop. Note that 22.Nd8? Qxf3 23.Nxe6+ Raxe6! costs White material.

22.Nd4	Qxf3
23.Nxf3	a4
24.Nd4	Bd7
25.Kf1	Rxe1+
26.Kxe1	c5

If this kicked Knight can reach a good square such as d5, White may equalize. Otherwise, the Black Rook will simply penetrate decisively at a2 or some other juicy invasion point.

27.Ne2	**Bf5**
28.Kd2	**g5!**
29.Nc1	

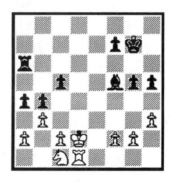

The Knight had no other way into play.

29...	**Kf6**
30.Nd3	**Bxd3!**

Converting one advantage into another. Now 31.Kxd3 Rd6+ leads to a lost King and pawn ending.

31.cxd3	**Ke5**
32.Re1+	**Kd6!**
33.h4!?	

A desperate bid for Rook activity.

33...	**axb3**
34.axb3	**Ra2+**

35.Ke3	gxh4
36.Rh1	Rb2

This creates the winning passed pawn.

37.Rxh4	Rxb3
38.Kd2?	Rb2+
39.Ke3	Rc2
40.Rxh5	b3

There is nothing to be done about ...b3-b2 and ...Rc1 now.

41.Rh6+	Kc7
42.Rf6	b2
43.Rxf7+	Kc6
44.Rf6+	Kb5

and Black won in a few moves.

7) Ziatsev-Dreev
Moscow 1989

1.e4	e5
2.Nf3	Nc6
3.Bb5	Nge7
4.Nc3	g6
5.d4	exd4
6.Nd5	Bg7
7.Bf4?!	Nxd5

| **8.exd5** | **Ne7** |

But not 8...Qe7+ because 9.Kf1! threatens to bring the king Rook to e1. The game Zaitsev-Vul, Planernaya 1983 went 9...a6 10.Ba4 b5 11.Bb3 Na5 12.Bg5 f6 13.Qd3 Kf8 14.Re1 and Black was in hot water.

9.d6

As we saw in Chapter Two, just because White gets to advance the d-pawn this far does not guarantee him an advantage.

9...	**cxd6**
10.O-O	**O-O**
11.Bxd6	**Re8**
12.Bc5	

Black was threatening 12...Qb6, attacking both Bishops. After 13.Be5 Bxe5 14.Nxe5 Nc6 or 13.Bg3 Qb6 White's compensation is not at all clear.

12...	**Qa5**
13.a4	**a6**
14.b4	

Forced, by the attack on the Bishops.

| 14... | Qc7 |
| 15.Bd3 | Nc6 |

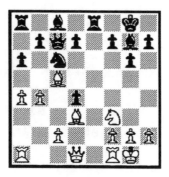

Black is finally ready to play 16...d6 and get his queenside developed.

16.a5	d6
17.Bb6	Qe7
18.Re1	Be6

White still has some pressure for the lost pawn but it isn't nearly enough. He now eases Black's task considerably with an unsound Exchange sacrifice.

19.b5	axb5
20.Bxb5	d3!
21.cxd3	

Hardly better was 21.Rb1 dxc2.

| 21... | Bxa1 |
| 22.Qxa1 | Qf8! |

23.Nd2	Bd5

After Black trades off a pair of Rooks he should be able to protect his kingside and convert his material edge.

24.Ne4	f5!
25.Nc3	

Not 25.Nf6+ Qxf6! 26.Rxe8+ Rxe8 27.Qxf6 Re1 mate.

25...	Rxe1+
26.Qxe1	Bf7
27.a6	

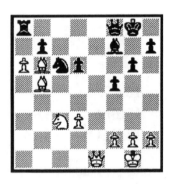

27...	Qc8
28.Bc4	Bxc4
29.dxc4	Qe8

White resigns.

CHAPTER FIVE

White's Alternatives at Move 10

1.e4	e5
2.Nf3	Nc6
3.Bb5	Nge7

We should note that while many players consider this a major strengthening of Black's play, there are also quite a few other players - e.g. Gata Kamsky, Vassily Smyslov–who still prefer 3...g6. It's your choice.

4.O-O	g6

Black can also convert the position into an improved version of the old Steinitz Defense, as the Swedish GM Tom Wedberg has done with 4...d6 5.c3 Bd7, e.g. 6.d4 Ng6 7.Nbd2 Be7 8.Re1 h6 9.Nc4 Bf6 10.Ne3 0-0 11.Bc4 Nh4 with approximate equality (Gufeld-Wedberg, Dortmund 1983).

5.c3	Bg7
6.d4	exd4

7.cxd4

Of course, 7.Nxd4 is out of character. Black gets a perfectly good game with 7...0-0 and a quick ...d7-d5. Rolf Schwarz even gives a line in which Black obtains a quick edge against 8.f4? Nxd4 9.cxd4 c6 and 10...Qb6.

7...   d5!

It is this important stroke that changes the nature of the center struggle. White can either allow his d4-pawn to become isolated (by 8.exd5 or by allowing 8...dxe4) or commit himself to the dubious 8.e5. The reason 8.e5 is doubtful is because of the vulnerability of the d4-pawn to Black's minor pieces after ...Bg4 and a later ...Bxf3, ...Nf5 and ...f7-f6.

For example, 8.e5 0-0 9.b3 Bg4 10.Bb2 f6 and Black won quickly in Nilsson-Villeneuve, Rilton Cup 1980-81 after 11.Nbd2 fxe5 12.Be2 e4. Hardly better is 11.exf6 Bxf6 12.Nbd2 Nxd4.

8.exd5   Nxd5

Now 9.Qe2+ is also played from time to time, e.g. 9...Be6 10.Bg5 Qd6 11.Nc3 and now 11...Nxc3?! 12.bxc3 0-0 13.Qd2 Na5 is a slight edge for White (Pedersen-Radulov, Burgas 1991). But Black does better with 11...0-0 and then 12.Ne4 Qb4 as in our main d) line below. His chances should be no worse than in the comparable 9.Re1+ position because White's d-pawn is more vulnerable with the Queen on e2, and Black can gain time with ...Rae8. See Illustrative Game 9.

When the Fianchetto Defense began its renaissance in the 1960's, this position was sharply re-evaluated. Previously it was thought that 9.Ne5 Qd6 10.Qa4 must favor White, and therefore Black's play since move five needed improvement.

However, the Bulgarian analyst Mechkarov found that Black's position was perfectly sound in this subvariation because of the pawn sacrifice 10...0-0!, e.g. 11.Nxc6 bxc6 12.Bxc6 Rb8 with excellent play against d4 and along the b-file. For example, 13.Qxa7? Qxc6! 14.Qxb8 Ba6! or 13.Nc3 Nb4! with superior chances for Black.

9.Re1+

The interpolation of 9.Bxc6+ bxc6 10.Bg5 Qd6 11.Re1+ Be6 (Wolff-I.Sokolov, Biel 1993) doesn't change matters–unless Black wants to try 10...Qb8!?.

9...Be6

Here lies a fork in the road. One move has gained precedence here but White can be readily tempted to try one of the three alternatives. They are a) 10.Ne5, b) 10.Ng5 and c) 10.Bxc6+. For the main line, 10.Bg5, see the final chapter.

a) 10.Ne5

10.Ne5

This natural move ensures that Black's queenside pawns will at least be messed up. The direct idea is to force Black to defend c6 in some time-consuming way.

10...   O-O!

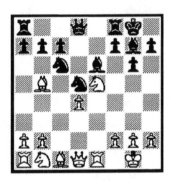

But he doesn't have to. This gambit is clearly better than 10...Qd6 11.Nd2! after which 12.Ne4 must gain White some advantage (11...0-0 12.Ne4 Qb4 13.Bxc6! bxc6 14.Nxc6 Qb6 15.Ne5 and White is a safe pawn up - Smyslov-De Grieff, Cienfuegos 1973).

11.Bxc6

Accepting the gambit is better by way of 11.Nxc6 bxc6 12.Bxc6 Rb8 13.Nc3. Then 13...Nb4 14.Be4 Qxd4 should grant Black fine play (but not 14...Bxd4 15.Qe2 Re8 16.Be3 c5? because of 17.Rad1 Nxa2 18.Bc6! and White won swiftly in Grabczewski-Lehmann, Eksjo 1974).

11...   bxc6
12.Nxc6

Turning the pawn down is safer but allows Black to obtain excellent chances with the maneuver of the Bishop to d5. For example, 12.Nd2 Ne7! 13.Qa4 Bd5 14.Nb3 Nf5 with splendid piece play.

This occurred in Rosentalis-I.Sokolov, Tilburg 1993, a game that lasted to move 28 but was decided almost immediately after 15.Bf4 Re8 16.Rad1 Nh4 17.f3 Qf6 18.Bg3 Nxg2! 19.Kxg2 Rxe5!.

12...	**Qd6**
13.Ne5	**Rfd8**

For the pawn Black has good pressure on the d-file and nice play on the light-colored squares. He has ...Nb4 or ...c7-c5 coming up.

14.Nd2

Of course not 14.Nc3 because of 14...Nxc3 and 15...Bxe5.

14...	**Nb6**

Even better may be 14...Ne7 and if 15.Ndf3, then 15...Nf5.

15.Ndf3	**Bd5**

Black had promising play in Veroci-Nikolau, Skopje 1972 (Illustrative Game 8).

After the discovery of 10.Ne5 0-0!, this entire variation gained a new lease on life. Another dangerous-looking White option at move 10 had previously lost its poison:

b) 10.Ng5

(after 1.e4 e5 2.Nf3 Nc6 3.Bb5 Nge7 4.O-O g6 5.c3 Bg7 6.d4 exd4 7.cxd4 d5 8.exd5 Nxd5 9.Re1+ Be6)

10.Ng5

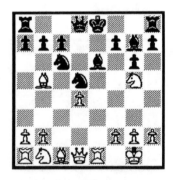

This was the other "book refutation" of the Fianchetto Defense in the period following World War II. But like so many such so-called refutations, it had not been seriously tested. Black's position may look porous after 11.Nxe6 but the e6-pawn will be no weaker than its opposite number at d4.

10...Qd6

Also untested is 10...0-0, allowing the Queen to reach h4 later on.

11.Nxe6

This is the whole point of White's play. After 11.Ne4 Qb4 Black has no problems.

11... fxe6
12.Qg4

White derives little from 12.Qa4 or 12.Nc3, both of which allow Black to castle into a balanced middlegame. The text is the only move that truly tests Black's opening.

12... O-O!

Of course: Black now threatens 13....Nxd4 and can meet the forcing 13.Rxe6 with 13...Qb4! (14.Bf1 Nxd4; 14.Bxc6 bxc6 and the d-pawn falls). Hardly better is 13.Qxe6+? Qxe6 14.Rxe6 Nxd4. Mechkarov's analysis continued 13.Bxc6 Qxc6 14.Qxe6+ (14.Rxe6?? hangs the c1-Bishop) Qxe6 15.Rxe6 Bxd4 and Black is already better.

We have one other side variation to consider and that is the immediate capture on c6.

c) 10.Bxc6+

(after 1.e4 e5 2.Nf3 Nc6 3.Bb5 Nge7 4.O-O g6 5.c3 Bg7 6.d4 exd4 7.cxd4 d5 8.exd5 Nxd5 9.Re1+ Be6)

10.Bxc6+

This frequently played move is suspect for the simple reason that is gives Black more possibilities of avoiding the main line than White. In fact, White's best chance is to transpose into main 10.Bg5 lines.

10...   bxc6

Now anything quiet on White's part should allow Black to complete his development and achieve a fine position. For example, 11.Nbd2 0-0 12.h3?! Nb4 13.Ne4 Re8 14.a3 Nd5 15.Bd2 Rb8 16.b3 Bf5 gave Black excellent play in Jun- Galliamova, World Junior 1988. Black won after penetrating on the light squares after 17.Ng3 Rxe1+ 18.Bxe1 Be6 19.Ne5 Qe8 20.b4 Nb6 21.Bc3 Rd8 22.Qf3 Bd5 and ...Na4.

11.Bg5

Now 11...Qd6 12.Nbd2 or 12.Nc3 will head into the main lines of the next chapter. For example, 12.Nbd2 0-0 13.Qc1 and Black can be lured

out of the main line with 13...Nb4? 14.Ne4 Qd5 15.Qd2! Na6 16.Nf6+ as in Kindermann-Mahmoud, Novi Sad 1990.

Black should accept the fact that in such an instance he must transpose into the next chapter with 13...Rfe8!. However, Black may have better at an earlier point thanks to White's inexact 10th move.

11...   Qb8!?

Obviously, Black would not have met 10.Bg5 with 10...Qb8 but here it places the Queen on a fine, active line.

12.Qd2   h6

This drives the Bishop off a good diagonal. Black does not want the Bishop available to defend the d4-pawn.

13.Bh4   O-O
14.Ne5   c5

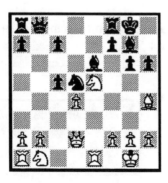

15.Nc3   Nxc3

Not 15...cxd4 because of 16.Nxd5 and 17.Nd7.

16.bxc3   cxd4

17.cxd4   Qb6

This is Wolff-Dreev, New York 1990. Black will reposition his Bishop to d5 and should be equal.

Illustrative Games

8) Veroci-Nikolau
Skopje 1972

1.e4	e5
2.Nf3	Nc6
3.Bb5	Nge7
4.c3	g6
5.d4	exd4
6.cxd4	d5
7.exd5	

In a comparable position from the Sicilian Defense (1.e4 c5 2.Nf3 g6 3.c3 Bg7 4.d4 cxd4 5.cxd4 d5) White almost always keeps his pawns together by pushing the e-pawn.

7...	**Nxd5**
8.O-O	**Bg7**
9.Re1+	**Be6**
10.Ne5	**O-O**

A natural gambit that, as mentioned above, gives Black a good game whether it is accepted or declined.

11.Bxc6	**bxc6**
12.Nxc6	**Qd6**
13.Ne5	**Rfd8**

Now 14.Nc4 Qb4 15.Nbd2 gets White's Knights into a tangle after 15...c5 or 15...Nb6.

14.Nd2	**Nb6**
15.Ndf3	**Bd5**
16.Bf4	**Qb4**

The Queen almost always finds its best counterplay on this square.

17.b3	**Bb7**
18.Rc1!	

Stopping 18...c5, attacking c7 and covering the invasion square at c3.

18...	Nd5
19.Bg3	Re8
20.Qc2	Bh6
21.Nd3	Qb6
22.Rcd1	Rad8

Both sides seem to have improved their position over the last five moves, but White is the only one to improve over the next five.

23.a3	Bg7
24.Be5	Bf8
25.Nc5	Bc6
26.h3	a5
27.Qc4	Bh6

28.Re4	Bb7
29.Rh4	Bf8
30.g4	Bc8

31.g5?!

A risky move designed to get a Knight to f6 via g4.

31...	**Bf5**
32.Re1	**Qc6**
33.Nh2	**Nb6**
34.Qc3	**Rd5**
35.Qg3	**Bg7**
36.f4?	**Rxd4!**

A blunder by White has allowed 37.Bxd4 Rxe1+ 38.Qxe1 Bxd4+ and 39...Qxc5.

37.Bxg7	**Kxg7**
38.Na4	**Rde4**
39.Rxe4	**Rxe4**
40.Qc3+	**Qxc3**
41.Nxc3	

The endgame is lost partly because of the extra Black pawn and partly because the h4-Rook is out of action.

41...	**Re3**
42.Nb5	**Nd5**
43.Nd4	**c5!?**
44.Nxf5+	**gxf5**
45.Rh6	**f6**
46.Rh5	**Nxf4**
47.gxf6+	**Kxf6**
48.Rxh7	**Rxb3**
49.h4	**c4**

50.Rc7	**c3**
51.a4	**Rb2**
52.Nf3	**c2 and Black won**

9) Timman-Spassky
Bugojno 1986

Probably no game did more to lend respectability to the 3...Nge7/3...g6 variation than this surprisingly easy victory by Black in a band of top GM's.

1.e4	**e5**
2.Nf3	**Nc6**
3.Bb5	**Nge7**
4.O-O	

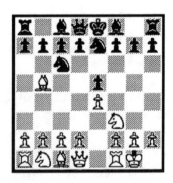

At the time, Spassky was also playing 3...g6 and meeting 4.c3 with 4...a6. His game with Chandler at Vienna 1986 diverged from normality with 5.Bxc6+?! dxc6 6.0-0 Bg7 7.d4 exd4 8.cxd4 and now 8...Bg4 looks fine for Black (9.Be3? c5). Black equalized without incident after 8...Ne7 9.Nc3 Bg4 10.Be3 0-0 11.h3 Bxf3 12.Qxf3 f5 although post-mortem analysis indicated 12...Bxd4 was perfectly all right.

4...	g6
5.c3	Bg7
6.d4	exd4
7.cxd4	d5
8.exd5	Nxd5
9.Bg5	

The insertion of this move before a check is just another order of moves. Of course, 9...Nde7? 10.Re1 only complicates Black's life.

9...	Qd6
10.Qe2+	Be6
11.Nbd2	O-O
12.Ne4	Qb4

This move does not threaten ...Qxb5 here (compared with 10.Re1+) but the Queen is nevertheless well-placed even after it is kicked by the a-pawn. Black must avoid 12...Qd7? 13.Nc5.

13.a3	Qa5
14.Bxc6	bxc6
15.Ne5	

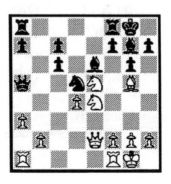

This is the beginning of a bad plan. But after 15.b4 Qb6 White ha
to acknowledge his Queen is misplaced and seek equality with 16.Qd2 an
17.Bh6.

15...	**Rae8!**
16.Rac1?	

After this, White is fighting for equality. He should have gotten hi
Queen off the hot file with 16.Qd2.

16...	**f6**
17.Nxc6	**Qb6**
18.Bd2	**Bd7!**

White likely underestimated the strength of this retreat. White i
now forced.

19.Nb4	**Qxd4**
20.Rc4	

Or 20.Nxd5 Qxd5 21.Qc4, which walks right into a lost endgame
(21...Qxc4 and 22...Bb5).

20...	**Qe5**
21.Nd3	**Qe7**
22.Qf3	**Bb5!**
23.Rd4	**c6**
24.Ng3	**Qd8**

The Queen has had quite an odyssey (...d6-b4-b6-d4-e5-e7-d8). Thi:
last retreat threatens 25...f5, an advance that would have failed badly here
(24...f5? 25.Rxd5).

25.a4	Ba6
26.Nb4	Qb6!
27.Rxd5	cxd5

Black's position is essentially won because the Exchange counts long before the extra pawn.

28.Nxa6	Qxa6
29.Qxd5+	Qe6
30.Qxe6+	Rxe6
31.Rc1	f5!

The advance of the f-pawn drives the Knight into hiding and sets up f2 as a target.

32.b4	f4
33.Nf1	Bd4
34.Rc4	Re4

Threatening 35...Bxf2+ and 36...Rxc4.

35.Kh1	Rfe8

36.h3

Even faster is the loss that follows 36.f3 Re1!.

36...	**Bxf2**
37.Rc6	**Re1!**
38.Bxe1	**Rxe1**
39.g4	**f3!**

A pretty finish that allows White to win a full piece (and not 39...Rxf1+ 40.Kg2).

40.Rc8+	**Kf7**

White resigns

CHAPTER SIX

Main Line 3...Nge7

1.e4	e5
2.Nf3	Nc6
3.Bb5	Nge7
4.O-O	g6

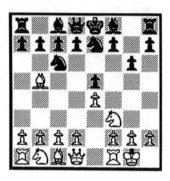

5.c3

It isn't seen often but 5...a6 is sometimes tried here. One benefit is that after 6.Ba4 Bg7 7.d4 exd4 8.cxd4 Black can continue 8...O-O, instead of 8...d5. Then 9.d5 can be answered by 9...b5 10.Bc2 Na5. This occurred in Kupreichik-Arkhipov, Munster 1991 and Black obtained the upper hand after 11.a4 b4 12.Nbd2 d6 13.Re1 c6 14.Nb3 Nxb3 15.Bxb3 Bg4 16.Bg5 c5 17.Rb1 h6 18.Bh4 g5 19.Bg3 f5.

5...	Bg7
6.d4	exd4
7.cxd4	

The rarity 7.Nxd4 occurred in the simultaneous exhibition game Muehrenberg-Lasker, Szcecin 1927. After 7...0-0 8.Bg5 h6 9.Bh4 the former world champion played 9...Qe8, not a bad idea.

7...	**d5**
8.exd5	**Nxd5**
9.Re1+	**Be6**
10.Bg5!	

Of all the forcing moves at White's disposal at move ten, this has endured the test of time.

10...   Qd6

Not at all a bad square for the Queen. It's chief drawback is that the Queen will be vulnerable to a kick from a Knight on e4 or c4.

11.Nbd2

This is regarded as the most exact sequence of moves. After 11.Nc3 Black has the additional option of 11...Nxc3 12.bxc3 0-0 and ...Bd5, with blockade play against the c3/d4 center.

From White's point of view the chief virtue of 11.Nc3 is the alternative plan of 11...0-0 12.Qd2 (rather than 12.Ne4).

Then 12...Rfe8 13.Bh6 appears to give White a small but secure edge. More promising is the blockade strategy (12...Nxc3 13.bxc3 Bd5 14.Bf4 Qd8 15.Qe2 a6 16.Bd3?! Qd7 with equality in Palatnik-Lehmann, 1976). However, White's failure to play Bxc6 so far gives Black another option – 12...Nce7!?.

For example:

1) 13.Ne4 Qb6 14.Bc4 Nf5 15.Nc5? Nxd4 obviously doesn't work. Not much better is 15.Rad1 h6!.

2) 13.Bc4 and now 13...f6 14.Bh4 Bf7 15.Bg3! favored White in Korneev-Kir. Georgiev, Torcy 1991. However, 13...Nf5! seems to improve significantly. Black's idea is 14...h6 and there doesn't appear to be a favorable way of meeting it, e.g. 14.Rac1 h6 15.Nxd5 Bxd5 16.Bf4 Qd7! 17.Ne5 Qd8 or 17.Bxd5 Qxd5 18.Rc5 Qxa2.

11...	O-O
12.Ne4	Qb4

13.Bxc6   bxc6
14.Qc1!

The discovery of this move nearly made 3...g6/3...Nge7 extinct more than 20 years ago. After 14...Bxd4? 15.Nxd4 Qxd4 16.Qxc6 White has simplified favorably and can exploit the enemy weaknesses on both wings (16...Qxb2 17.Rad1 Qb6 18.Qc1 f6 19.Bh6!).

But there are improvements. Among them is 14...Rab8 15.b3 Bf5, a kind of gambit (16.Qxc6 Qb5 17.Qxb5 Rxb5) and our main line.

14...   Rfe8

Now 15.Bh6 offers no chance for more than equality (and, in fact, may favor Black).

15.Bd2

This has been treated as the main line for the past five years but there is no clear evidence that White cannot use this retreat more usefully after some preparatory moves. For example, 15.h3 Rab8 16.b3 Bf5 and now 17.Bd2 Qb6 18.Nc5 h5 19.Ne5 led to a slight edge for White in Wolff-I.Sokolov, Biel 1993 (19...Rbd8 20.Qa3 Re7 21.Rac1 Rde8 followed, and eventually the game ended in a draw).

15...   Qb6

Black stays in a position to meet 16.Qc5 with 16...Qxb2. An intriguing alternative to the text is 15...Qb5 and if 16.Ne5 Bf5 17.Ng3, then 17...Ne7!. This was a successful policy in Gelfand-Dreev, Moscow 1989 after 18.Bh6 Bxh6! 19.Qxh6 f6 and Black was already a bit better. See Illustrative Game 11.

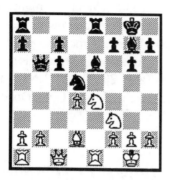

16.Nc5	Bf5
17.Ne5	

And here 17...Bxe5? 18.dxe5 must favor White (18...Nb4 19.Bg5! Nc2 20.Nd7! Bxd7 21.Qxc2). Black must use his Rooks on the center files and await events. He can part with his g7-Bishop when the time is right.

17... Rad8

Alexey Dreev has tried 17...Re7 here and that is not a bad move. After 18.Nb3 Bxe5 19.dxe5 Rae8 the Rooks become noisy (20.Na5 c5 21.b3 Bd3 22.Nc4. Oll-Dreev, Soviet Championship 1989 with advantage to White).

But in the last line, 21...Nb4! improves Black's chances measurably – 22.Nc4 Qc6 23.Bxb4 cxb4 24.Qe3 with a very slight advantage for White.

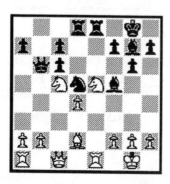

The position is deceptive. White's Knight are a bit more impressive than dangerous. Black can unravel them with care, e.g. 18.a3 Nf6 19.Qc4 Rf8 20.Bc3 Ng4! or 20.b4 Ne4!. In the latter variation, Black can simplify down to a heavy piece middlegame in Which his chances are no worse than White's. For illustration (after 20...Ne4): 21.Nxe4 Rxd4 22.Qxc6 Bxe5 or 21.Bc3 Bxe5! 22.dxe5 Nxc5 23.bxc5 Qb5 (Donchev-Radulov, Bulgaria 1991).

Illustrative Games

10) Chandler-Boudhiba
Lucerne 1989

1.e4	e5
2.Nf3	Nc6
3.Bb5	Nge7

Strictly speaking, this is the ancient Cozio Defense, which Bent Larsen has tried to revive with ...Ng6 and ...Bc5.

| 4.c3 | g6 |
| 5.d4 | exd4 |

6.cxd4	d5
7.exd5	Nxd5
8.O-O	Bg7
9.Re1+	Be6
10.Bg5	Qd6
11.Nc3	O-O
12.Qd2	

This plan earned a solid reputation in the late 1980's. White prepares to exchange off Bishops after Bh6.

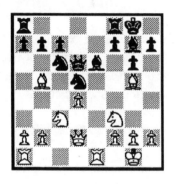

12...	Rfe8

As mentioned earlier, 12...Nxc3 is a leading alternative here. Now with 13.Bh6 Bh8 14.h3 White retains a slight edge.

13.h3	Nxc3!
14.bxc3	Bd5

Note that 15.Nh2 allows the cheapo 15...Bxg2! 16.Kxg2 Qd5+.

15.Bf4   Rxe1+!

An important interpolation because the desirable 16.Rxe1 allows 16...Qa3! and White may even be in a bit of trouble, e.g. 17.Bxc7 Qxa2 18.Qf4 Qb3. Black can obtain a serious edge if he gains a queenside majority by trading his c7-pawn for the one at c3 or a2.

16.Nxe1   Qd8

In fact, 16...Qa3 would have been a good try here (17.Bxc7 Rc8 and Black should favorably regain a pawn).

17.Rc1	a6
18.Bf1	b5

This secures d5 for the Bishop and c4 for a Black Knight but gives up c5 to a White Knight.

19.Nd3	Na5
20.Re1	Nc4
21.Qe2	a5
22.Nc5	h5

23.Qc2

White can penetrate to e7 but after 23.Qe7 Qxe7 24.Rxe7 c6–or
...b5-b4 immediately–he stands perfectly well.

23...	**Bf8**
24.Qc1	**c6**
25.Bg5	**Qc7**
26.Bd3	

After the game White noted that 26.Bxc4! would have given him
an edge (26...bxc4 27.Ne4).

26...	**Nd6**
27.a4	**Bc4**
28.Bc2	**Re8**
29.Bf6	**Bg7**

The exchange of Bishops and Rooks reduces matters to a fairly even
endgame.

30.Bxg7	**Kxg7**
31.Rxe8	**Nxe8**
32.Be4	**Nf6**
33.Bf3	**Bd5**
34.Be2	

Black seeks, and White avoids, the exchange of Bishops that would
allow Black greater use of the light squares.

34...	**Nd7**

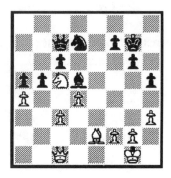

35.axb5

After this the position peters out to a draw. But on 35.Qa3 Nxc5 36.Qxc5 Black obtains counterplay with the a-pawn he creates via 36...bxa4 37.c4 Be4 38.d5 Qe5! 39.Qxc6 a3, as White pointed out.

35...	Nxc5
36.dxc5	cxb5
37.Bxb5	Qxc5
38.c4	Be6
Draw	

In view of 39.Qc3+ Kh7 40.Qxa5? Bxc4! and Black wins.

11) Gelfand-Dreev
Moscow 1989

1.e4	e5
2.Nf3	Nc6
3.Bb5	Nge7
4.O-O	g6
5.c3	Bg7

6.d4	exd4
7.cxd4	d5
8.exd5	Nxd5
9.Re1+	Be6
10.Bxc6+	bxc6
11.Bg5	

A minor change in move order from 10.Bg5.

11...	Qd6
12.Nbd2	O-O
13.Qc1	Rfe8
14.Ne4	Qb4
15.Bd2	Qb5

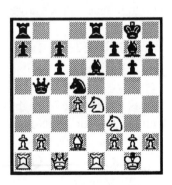

In a way it makes good sense for the Queen to be on a light square, rather than b6.

| 16.Ne5 | Bf5 |
| 17.Ng3 | |

Afterwards Gelfand said 17.Nc5, as in comparable 15...Qb6 positions, was correct. He may have counted here on 17...Bc8 18.Qxc6, which leads to a clear White edge.

17...   Ne7!
18.Bh6?

And this is a bad plan. With 18.b3 or 18.Nxf5 White's game is perfectly all right; he just has no advantage..

18...   Bxh6
19.Qxh6   f6!

Not falling for 19...Qxb2? 20.Nxc6! and then 20...Nxc6 21.Nxf5 gxf5 22.Qxc6 with a clear superiority. After 19...f6 the Knight lacks a good retreat (20.Nf3 Qxb2) but 20.Qh4! (and then 20...fxe5 21.Rxe5 Nd5 22.Nxf5 gxf5 23.Rae1) was found to reduce Black's advantage.

20.Re3!?   fxe5
21.Rxe5   c5!

Now if White piles up on the e7-Knight with 22.Rae1, Black will keep the upper hand with 22...Qd7 or 22...Nd5.

22.Qg5   Qd7
23.Rae1

Gelfand also pointed out the cute defense 23.Nh5 h6!! 24.Qxg6 gxh5 25.Qg5+ Kf7 26.Rae1 Qd6 and Black wins.

23...   Nc6
24.Nxf5!   Nxe5
25.Nh6+   Kg7
26.dxe5   Qd8!

Now 27.Qc1 Qh4 wins for Black without much trouble.

27.h4!	**Qxg5**
28.hxg5	**Rab8**

In time trouble Black misses the more exact 28...Rad8 and then...

29.Re2	**Rb4**
30.f3	**Rd4**
31.Ng4	**Red8?**

...he puts the other Rook on d8 rather than take proper precautions against the e-pawn. After 31...Kf7 32.Rc2 c4 or 32.Nf6 Red8 Black has good winning chances when his King reaches e6.

32.e6!	**Re8**
33.Re5	**Re7**
34.Rxc5	

White has recovered thanks to Black's miscue and can eke out a draw.

34...	**Rd1+**

35.Kh2	**Rd6**
36.Ne5	**Rdxe6**
37.f4	**Rd6**
38.Ra5	**c6**
39.Ra6!?	

At least a draw. In fact, as Gelfand pointed out, 39.b4! would give White some winning chances thanks to the clumsiness of the Black Rooks.

39...	**Rb7**
40.b3	**h6**
41.gxh6+	**Kxh6**
Draw	

NOTES

NOTES

NOTES

NOTES